END OF PART ONE

First published in 2006 by
The Dedalus Press
13 Moyclare Road
Baldoyle
Dublin 13
Ireland

www.dedaluspress.com

ISBN 1 904556 61 2 (bound)
ISBN 1 904556 57 4 (paperback)

Dedalus Press titles are represented in North America
by Syracuse University Press, Inc., 621 Skytop Road,
Suite 110, Syracuse, New York 13244, and in the UK by
Central Books, 99 Wallis Road, London E9 5LN

Printed and bound in the UK by Lightning Source,
6 Precedent Drive, Rooksley, Milton Keynes MK13 8PR

Design and typesetting by Pat Boran
Cover image: 'Man on wire' © Photoganda Inc.

The Dedalus Press receives financial assistance from
An Chomhairle Ealaíon / The Arts Council, Ireland.

END OF PART ONE

Gerry Murphy

To Landless,
an honour and a pleasure
to be on the same bill
with you,

[signature]

June 24th 2017
FARM GATE

Dedalus

ACKNOWLEDGEMENTS

Grateful acknowledgement is made to the editors of the following in which a number of these poems, or versions of them, originally appeared:

Café Review, Carapace, Compost, Cúirt Annual 2004, De Brakke Hond, The Irish Times, New Orleans Review, Poetry Ireland Review, The SHOp and *Southword.*

For Seán Lucy

Contents

from *Extracts from The Lost Log-Book of Christopher Columbus* (1999)

from *Torso of an Ex-Girlfriend* (2002)

New Poems: *The Psychopathology of Everyday Life*

Master of the Epigram

Foreword by John Montague

When I began to read Gerry Murphy
I saw the statue of Lenin levitate slightly
As it saw Gerry Murphy...

O ne of the things Gerry Murphy has done in his work is to create an attractive persona, a middle-aged bachelor living on Melville Terrace, Military Hill, overlooking Cork. *Multum in parvo*: his technical achievement is to adapt the classical epigram to his little city-state. And to modern life in general, with the Oedipus of Epidarus shrunk to a pungent salutation, 'Yo, muthafucker!' ('Oedipus in Harlem'). Or Genesis distilled to three lines: 'God falls apart, / awareness glitters in the burnished deserts of obsidian, / an astonished sky contemplates an astonished ocean.'

Lenin haunts the volume's strange vision of a terror-ridden world, or end of world: 'The dream-map shows / unrelieved desolation, / a cheerful oblivion / smoothing over a charred landscape...' Perhaps Murphy is influenced by Lenin's famous comment, 'The misfortune of the Irish is that they rose prematurely, when the European revolt of the proletariat had not yet matured.'

Love is a constant, with a litany of loves, often bearing real names, a daring move. Catullus and e. e. cummings combine in these offbeat homages, where the only surety is tenderness. 'I could pass my hands softly / across your aching shoulders, / easing tension, / inventing calm / erasing history.'

What makes Murphy unique among his contemporaries is his curious integrity, the way he has created an aesthetic out of nearly nothing, *ex nihilo*. But there is much skill behind his lightness of touch, with adaptations of Seferis, Lorca, Milosz and many others. Indeed he sums up the whole problem of translation in a typical epigram: 'Stark moonlit silence / the brindled cat is chewing / the nightingale's tongue.' And perhaps his most hauntingly bittersweet lyric is an adaptation from the Spanish of Gongora: 'Fortune presents gifts / according to her whims, / not according to the book. / She blinds the prophet in one eye / and gives the village idiot second sight. / When you expect whistles, it's flutes, / when flutes, whistles.'

And as a last sally, what if you are heading home from an all-night binge? 'The late worm / slithers homeward / after a night / on the beer-spattered tiles, / only to meet / the flashing beak / of the stone-cold sober / early bird.'

End of Part One

Poem in One Breath

Not that you
would notice
but every time
you pass
up the corridor
Lenin's statue
levitates slightly
to get a better view
of the remarkable ease
with which you fill
curved space.

Love Poem

Any other time but now
a brass band would be
appropriate—
welcome, even.
I am trying to remember
where it was I first
met you and why
I insulted you and how
it is that I have come
to admire you so much—
love, even.
I think they're going to play
A Nation Once Again.
Shit anyway!—
fuck, even.

Ethiopia, The Wilderness and everything else

No doubt
your heart has told you
how it is with me now—
the wilderness and all that—
since you left for Ethiopia.
Well, assuming the secret police
do not reveal themselves
within the next few days
to investigate the bombing
of the Cathedral
(if they do, I will tell them everything),
and assuming you return
safely from Addis Ababa,
remember that if you want
someone to meet you at the airport
or someone to lie out with you
on the landing strip
until the spinning world
spins out,
if you want to talk
about the end
or for that matter the beginning
of the Universe
before the cleaning women
move in,
then give me a shout—
yahoo?

Because there is ice,
at least on high ground,
I am worried
(have you sent a St. Bernard for your sheep?)
that you might not get here safely

or in one piece
(if anything does drop off, bring it with you—
I have a friend in micro-surgery),
that one of your reindeer might slip
in a reckless attempt
to overtake a troop-carrier
outside Guatemala City
and fall under
its huge grinding wheels,
red nose flaring,
bells jangling uselessly.

The dream-map shows
unrelieved desolation,
a cheerful oblivion
smoothing over a charred landscape,
except for the Temple of Diana,
intact, far out into the desert
next to a hamburger-stand.

Waking up to 1 below,
I send for Amundsen,
I check all the instruments,
jiggling the mercury,
it's somehow reassuring.
I begin to think of you
in short concentrated bursts,
fiercer and fiercer
as the ice floes snap shut
the cruel straits.
Imagine it,
opening my mouth and saying:
"I want you here forever."

Greetings
from the wilderness.
The flowers
I kept from the blast
are withering for want
of water I cannot
extract from the rock
I struck thrice with my head.
But oh,
to be with you,
to be with you,
to be with you.

A Note at The End

There's nothing else for it
but to dream steadily,
to concentrate on a spot
below your left earlobe
towards the nape
of your neck,
leave the front door open,
a light in the hall,
enough room in the bed
and hope to wake
with your sleepy ghost
snug beside me.

Suite for Ms. G.

You have to be quick
to get out:
here's a snapshot
of lush countryside
after Summer rain.
Someone may be kind enough
to take you out
into lush countryside
or (wait for it)
into the rainforest.

In this dream
I am hugging you close.
My head is bowed
to kiss your collar-bone,
my tongue slick
between your breasts.
Nothing like love,
nothing at all like love.

Waking,
I find myself
whispering your name
over and over
into my armpit.
I detect
a certain delirium,
a whiff of swamp-fever.
I soon tire of this
and put the kettle on.
All right!
I love you—
fucksake.

Have you any idea
how much sleep
I have gained
since I put you
on the pedestal with Lenin?
This places you
six inches below
and a little to the right
of my constant adoration.
Ah… but look,
over there…
trees and shrubs and flowers.
Comfortable?

Fuck this rain!
Fuck it again.
I thought we might be allowed
a brief respite,
a small crack in the clouds,
a spot of sunshine
to spark the sodden bee.
But no,
nothing doing.
Well this means
getting my bib wet,
fuck it—
this means war!

After the rain,
if I meet you
in Patrick Street,
will you rest
your forehead
for a moment
against my chest
and tell me

where the most
interesting exhibition is
and then kiss me
briskly on each cheek?

This is it—
your last warning—
if you don't
come over here
right now
and expose
your neck,
all of your neck
down to the small of your back,
I'll…

No I won't.

A Poem to be Read on a Moonlit Night Outside a Police Station

Not that I mind so much now
but should anything happen
to Western Democracy—
perish the thought—
before we have had a chance
to walk along the riverbed
on a warm Summer's evening
without being instantly surrounded
by armoured personnel carriers,
demanding attention, respect,
even affection for the President,
I will never forgive myself
for not telling you in time
how much I do, in fact, love you.

It's not that I miss you very much
(after all, there are plenty of people here
who would be onlytoowilling...)
in fact, there is probably a party
going on this very minute to which
I have been invited but due to
a breakdown in communications
resulting from the State of Emergency,
I don't as yet know of—
the party that is.

Not a red guard in sight
as we left the party
to walk home
under a full moon
along the river.
Not a priest awake

to take to task
about the dwindling
kingdom of heaven.
You and me embracing…
no god,
no merlin,
no lenin.

A Poem for Herr Speer with Hitherto
Unpublished Historical Details

In Hitler's arsehole
there was a small trapdoor,
to be opened in the event
and only in the event
of a final breakthrough
on the Eastern Front.
Inside, you would find
a secret tunnel
which would lead you out
under Berlin
into a heavily-concealed,
well-stocked cave
with all the facilities necessary
to encourage the establishment
of a government in exile.

What more could any fascist want?

A Complete History of The Hot Club de France

So as not to leave
anything unsaid, understated
or lying wounded in a corner
without recourse to medical attention;
in order to clear up
any outstanding mysteries
pertaining to the burning of Persepolis,
and just for the record
I have compiled a list—
get this down quick!

I am quite fond of you
and though you are forever
passing dressed and half-dressed
before my mind's fevered eye,
I have taken extraordinary care
not to place
even the slightest weight of admiration
on your lovely young shoulders.
I have been visiting you
constantly of late out of a sense
of extreme delight in your company
and place myself completely
at your disposal
all hours of the day,
all hours of the night.
I can no more forget you now
than forget myself,
though I am perfecting
several techniques in Yoga
and related disciplines
to develop a proficiency in levitation
which should, in good time,

enable me to transcend
this utterly base obsession,
imparting in the process a beatific blandness
which would be the envy of all my friends.

I have no wish
nor do I foresee a time when I would wish
to transcend this glorious obsession—
fuck off, Buddha,
fuck off.

Vision at Knock

for Paul Durcan

A figure,
perhaps John the Evangelist
and behind John
an altar
and on the altar
a lamb
and behind the lamb
a cross
and behind the cross
a wet gable wall
and behind the wall
a poky interior
and behind
this poky interior
a dismal view of the countryside
and beyond
this dismal view of the countryside
and a little to the right
the Cathedral of Minsk
and behind
the Cathedral of Minsk:
Stalin
laughing.

A Small Fat Boy Walking Backwards

I should have kept right on going
(smiling inwardly perhaps)
and said nothing
until I was able to confide
in a policeman.
After all it could have been merely
a child's reaction to the probability
of imminent global annihilation
or to the fluctuating price of gold,
or was it rumours of a coup in Greece
which troubled his young socialist heart?

Anyway I couldn't resist inquiring
as to why he chose such an unorthodox
mode of conveyance with such grim determination.
He told me to fuck off.

Yet consider, if you will, the possibility
that when the Universe loses
its tremendous momentum of expansion
and begins to collapse back
slowly on itself,
Time, Sex, Space, Previous Existence, Mensheviks, Goethe, Tax
Evasion, Syphilis, Early Byzantium, Hitler, Detergent, Cyprus, Mozart,
The I.R.A., Stephen Hawking, The Boston Tea Party, Absolutely
Enormous Breasts, Jupiter, Sperm Banks, Papal Infallibility, Dante,
Mobile Colonic Irrigation, Coca Cola, Women's Soccer, John Quincy Adams,
Anarcho-Syndicalism, Treblinka, 1065, Under Milk Wood, Athlete's Foot,
Particle Accelerators, John Brown's Body and A Partridge in a Pear Tree
will reappear faster and faster in final reverse order.

Last Surrealist Litany of The Twentieth Century

Go

your hair
which is afro-style
autumnal
deep wood long walks
at evening
your forehead
which is somewhat obscured
by afro-style
autumnal
deep wood long walks
at evening
type hair
your eyes
which are blue
or grey
or green
which are deep
as the sky
or if you must
the sea
your lips
which are as lips go
oh shirley temple
your lips
your neck
which should be
turret of ivory
columnar marble
miracle of steel
would hold in suspense
without difficulty

the san francisco bridge
your breasts
which are hot and glossy
and fit neatly
into your bra
the persistent dream
of you swimming
warm glistening curves
rippling under
a red swimsuit
on the first
all woman expedition
to the source
of the amazon
your thighs
of natalya kuchinskaya
such thighs
begin quietly at the throat
then open out
onto a spectacular view
of mount fujiyama
inviting a long historic trek
around the poles
of your nipples
across the hot moonscape
of your belly
towards the cool caravanserai
of your navel
to create the legend
of your vulva
smooth
powdered
smothered in jewellery
between the slow descent
of your legs

stop.

Twenty-One Words for The Security Council

It's a pity
the Earth isn't flat.
You could line the poor
along the edges
and machine-gun them
into the abyss.

Dream Sequence

Actually, nothing much,
just trying to sleep
by exorcising your warm
tingling ghost with thoughts
on Left Wing Communism
and the Kronstadt Mutiny.
If I could get this tossing—
no—
if I could get this
turning right,
I would eventually
wind up in your arms.

What if I were to go out
right now without consulting
my barometer, nor for that matter,
my necromancer,
travel across the rooftops
until I came to your dimly lit
skylight and let myself down
on a rope of Soviet flags
into your empty bed?

Fucksake,
stay up a little later in future
in the sudden event of a serious need
for a disco after a week-end
of selective assassination.
Fucksake,
at least pretend you understand
all this jangling madness
to be heavy jazz.
Inevitably,
snow from the north-east,

wrap up well—
fucksake.

A little less hurry
and I would be kissing your armpits;
a little less vagueness
and I would be nuzzling your crotch;
a little more emphasis
and I would be standing outside
your window tonight
with a six-pack, a pet leopard
and a recently discovered photograph
of the young Stalin.

I suppose I must provide you
with endless amusement
by walking home with Dr. Goebbels
every night.
Well, if you knew how much practice
it takes and the serious operation
I underwent on my hip
just to keep in step
with that dear little man,
you might be a trifle more understanding.

Don't go to sleep just yet
because I am on my way over
with a letter from Hitler,
in which he apologises most sincerely
for his unfortunate treatment
of you know who, you know when,
but insists that, should you be prepared
to forgive and forget,
he will come out from hiding
in the Andean foothills
and join your mother's
anti-communist front.

Almost dawn,
I would make room in the bed
if you were to come bounding
across the rooftops
and appear at the window,
dripping with rain, smelling of ivy
and swearing that if only I could
speak it, you would certainly understand
Swahili.
Eventually I will say something
utterly original
about your perfectly exquisite body
but for now
I want nothing more
than the death of King Arthur
laid squarely at the door
of the Saigon Military Police.

If you are reading this
in a railway station in Ecuador
under a wafer-thin moon in 1953
with all the time in the world
since the coup has delayed indefinitely
all trains in and out of Quito,
don't argue with the station master,
just relax,
for though the military appear courteous,
it would not trouble them to shoot
one foreign national
despite the attention of the International Press.
Incidentally,
I did kiss you as you left.
If you cannot and wish to remember it,
just draw your fingers once, softly,
across your lips.

And finally,
the singing of nightingales,
the strumming of lutes,
the sobbing of castrati
outside your window every night
comes to you courtesy
of Radio Moscow's new personal service
for Heroes of the Revolution.

Still Point

Sometime,
when you are tired
of all that is advertised
as a must
for the Modern Woman,
you could drop everything
(even the Waterford Crystal)
and call up here.
We could have a long conversation,
over a dry white wine,
concerning migratory seabirds.
I could pass my hands softly
across your aching shoulders,
easing tension,
inventing calm,
erasing history.

Part of a Poem to Celebrate Your Next Birthday

Keeping
one eye open
for
minorfluctuationsinthepropertymarket,
keeping the heart
pent up for Spring,
I watch you swim,
I calculate your trade value.

I could, of course, ask you out:
into the rain forests,
the Jovian ice-fields,
the fresh air?
Onto the lunar surface,
the veldt,
the sea floor?
Is there anything
in particular
you desire?

There's nothing here for you,
at least...
If it's all the same to you...
nothing you could take home
to mother...
I am developing
a fixed obsession
for your navel
...except perhaps
a view of the river
and floating quietly
thereupon...
a small passion for your breasts

...a few dead priests,
though (dare I say it?)...
the hots (the very hots)
for your vulva
...(Yes?)...
and a cool detached admiration
for your legs...
not enough?

Even if it is
only a matter of days
before the commencement
of nuclear (oh shit) hostilities—
are you digging in
under your Swiss bank account?—
and even if Castro is dead—
sorry I mean Lenin—
at least it's Spring
the birds are sing

ing, there is a sharp bluecold wind
streaking in from the Atlantic,
and if you search carefully
along the edge of this poem
or, if you will, along the edge
of the Arctic Circle,
you will find references
to your exquisite face,
the pert delight
of your breasts,
the lovely slow curves
of your hips,
the southern tip
of South America,
that sort of thing.

Of course,
if you are saving yourself
for an Associate Professor
and would rather not
be identified too closely
with this surrealist excess,
lest it be discovered
at some future date
and brought up
before a Senate Sub-Committee hearing
on the suitability
of your husband (now a Professor)
as ambassador to Papua New Guinea,
just say so,
I can take a hint.

News from The Home Front

Mr. Bourke
is beginning to have his doubts
about Democracy.
Nothing to worry us in this,
after all Mr. Bourke
in his present position
poses no significant threat
to Democracy
and even if he were to go out
into the streets right now
canvassing support
for his New Revolutionary
Post Democratic Peoples' People
Party (at Margaret's place)
he would probably attract
little more than the same old gang
of walking wounded from the "Long Valley"
and possibly the motorised SS
with six-packs.

Me?
I just dream of sleeping with you,
sleeping without you.

A Question for Mick Murphy

I wonder if you had lived longer
would you have gone to America,
to watch the "home runs"
streak out over the cheering stands,
rather than hanging on desperately
to an oscillating signal from the wireless,
carrying DiMaggio's magic
clear across the Atlantic?

Something Else

sometimes walking
sometimes waiting
for a bus sometimes
for a political solution
wanting you more
often
than
not.

it's nothing
(the C.I.A.?)
safety first,
appearing at the unlit window
with an automatic rifle
(a civil war reaction)
I am quite fond of you

something else

if people are whispering
if people are forming a queue
if people are drowning themselves
so what
there is a night wind from Zanzibar
inching across my skin…
it is as if…

it's not the government—
they are in exile in Cuba
it's not the secret police—
they are in the attic,
wrapped individually
in newspaper

in a small cardboard box
it's not the army—
they are in the garden
levelling a statue of Lenin
to clear a way for a new road
which will make it possible
for lightly-armoured vehicles
to pursue mounted terrorists
it's not the weather—
continuing dry spells
with occasional thundery showers
it's not the clergy—
they are either dead or scattered
though reports of continued resistance
are coming down from the hills
it's not angst
it's not imperialism (not exactly)
it's missing you
from the trenches
from the street fighting
from the justified slaughter
of those so-called innocents
from the small hours
the last five minutes before midnight
the weight of your weary arms
along my shoulders
your cheek pressed softly
against my cheek
making tentative propaganda.

however
fond of you I might become
there will always be a view
between cooldark
evergreen trees
down to the river
beyond an open window

in the early Spring
or Summer
beyond my warmest regard
for your heart and mind
beyond regret beyond speculation
beyond snow beyond isolation
beyond delirium beyond revisionism
beyond fervour beyond revolution
beyond counter-revolution
beyond complete and utter quiet
beyond the front door
of the police station in Saigon
which has just been dynamited
off its hinges and cannot
close behind you.

On His Deathbed My Grandfather Warns Me
against Literature

"Books!"
snarled my grandfather,
"are a bloodless substitute for life."
The thick blue ink of his veins
clotting happily
into commas, semi-colons
and colons,
towards a sudden and glorious
full stop.

Short Jazz Piece

Without so much as a nod
to the havoc you create
you climb from the pool
and walk to the dressing room
a thin wisp of cloth caught
in the lovely swell of your buttocks
riding the smooth power of your hips
exciting a rampant snarl of lust
my heart skips

a beat—
two if you like.

Part of a Poem to Celebrate Your Next Birthday

As soon as you came in
I wanted to celebrate hugely
I wanted to leap into the small
blue vase and send the daffodils
flying I wanted to prostrate myself
along the bar in homage to your svelte
perfection I wanted to convince
the barman of the absolute significance
of the moment I wanted the Carnival of Rio
to emerge exuberant from the toilet
I wanted to invent vertigo
I wanted to exude Revolution
I wanted to sprout red flags
I wanted to bequeath the entire
left side of my body to the people
of Leningrad I wanted to depart
there and then for anywhere in Siberia
within warm and easy reach
of your fully-extended arms.

Sweet Spring Rain

Haydn's *London* Symphony
is up and running in the next room,
the second movement
already swelling the air
with glad Northern light.
Spring continues its steady green push
in the municipal shrubberies
according to strict municipal arrangement.
I am sitting by an open window
overlooking the lower harbour,
thinking of you,
watching the steady glare of sunlight
glazing the marshlands,
thinking of

I suppose it's too late to join
the Foreign Legion to forget exactly
why I find you so attractive
and why you persist in my dimly-
lit dreams like a neon ghost
and why I scan the streets
this early Spring
for the least purple sign
of the purple jacket
of your purple approach
in purple vain
and why I wake at 4 a.m.
with the idea of sending you flowers,
apples and long sunlit avenues
steaming after fresh April rain
and why I go to sleep
with every intention
of dreaming about someone else

as someone else
and why the encyclopaedia of longing
is open at your face, your name,
and why this end of the world poem
is not that at all,
at all...

Still wrapped in your dream embrace,
still afloat in the liquid pleasure
of your imagined presence,
I go down into the city
to shake off this disturbing exhilaration
amongst the stern bustling crowds
only to find your remarkable face
informing the features
of so many hitherto
unremarkable women.

At this stage
I could say yellow
and expect to see yellow,
I could say pink
and this entire area
would become shrill with pink.
As it is,
the immediate landscape is bathed
in a warm red-yellow glow,
the evening breeze is translating
deep green fully-leafed conversations
for the trees along the river bank,
and Sirius alone is flashing,
diamond-sharp in a mauve sky.
I might say I miss your presence
or, more to the point,
the lovely effect of your presence
here at the edge of the known world,

the wilderness stretching far away
towards unknown Ringaskiddy,
fabled, many-spired Cobh,
the impenetrable dream-forests at Currabinny
and the fretful uncharted seas beyond.

If I have fallen into
or under your spell
then at least
I have trailed a rope-ladder
behind me all the way down.
If you have seen me
little of late
it is because
I have been impersonating
MacCurtain Street
and the entire length of Summerhill
to discreetly observe you passing,
relishing every step.
If I am enthralled,
if I am enraptured,
if I am entranced by your loveliness,
then I am not entirely disarmed:
I keep a small automatic in my hip pocket
and a grenade under each lapel
just in case.

Clarke's Bridge Vignette

for Mary Gilleece

Slightly amused
and as lovely as
the ink-black river
turning far below,
you paused to reminisce.
Suddenly shy
and as awkward as
the snarling traffic on the bridge,
I found myself,
or rather lost myself,
staring at your feet.

On Dunkettle Bridge

Quiet again
as the planet springs back
in the wake
of the Cobh Express,
the evening sun
gleaming by rail
into the city.

Rio de la Plata and All That...

Watching the bus
until it finally appears,
a shiny red speck
trailing a small cloud of dust
along the edge of the desert,
until it wavers
and suddenly dissolves
in the shimmering heat,
until your kiss dries out,
leaving a brisk ring of salt
tingling on my cheek.

Or,
I could be in North Africa,
searching furiously for this poem
under a sheaf of police reports
that mention your arrival
in Paris in the company
of three Middle Eastern terrorists
who are already under sentence
of death in Tunisia
where I missed you yesterday
the day after you left.

In the midst of all this
I felt an overwhelming desire
to see you,
even if it meant leaving the party,
which, you will admit, is a lot to expect,
especially since I was the centre of attraction
and moreover since the Swedish woman
in the corner actually winked at me.
At least I think she did.

Anyway she was Swedish
or most certainly Dutch.
Well, there was a lot of smoke
and a mad crush of bodies.

It might be said
that I miss you a little.
I dream of you nightly,
I crave your breasts,
your warm mouth,
your smooth vulva
opening into slick cave of delight,
the perfect fit of your buttocks:
tight,
tight,
tight.

As for your mother,
I suppose I could threaten her
with the Peoples' Republic of China
or a simple, low-yield nuclear device
detonated in the kitchen
or, for that matter,
I could say that there was a barn
blown down in County Wicklow
with sudden morbid emphasis
thereby arousing her curiosity
if not her respect.
Of course if I were a doctor
or an engineer
or even a teacher…
But no,
that would be scraping the bottom
of the barrel, that would be turning it
over to scrape underneath.

Still, the tea was nice
and the cake?
Just scrummy.

Later on, much later on,
I learned that there really was a party
in full swing in Buenos Aires
that very night before you left
and, if we had not been so wrapped up
in ourselves we might have heard the sounds
of revelry drifting down the River Plate,
out into the South Atlantic,
up around the Azores,
over the cliffs at Myrtleville
and through the open window
at the bottom of your bed.
But, there you are,
we had obviously floated too far up
into the Seventh Level of Heaven
to notice the bedraggled Argentinian
with the party hat
clambering over the sill.

Feminist on Beach in Dress-Suit

Dear Superman,
I found your condom
on the beach this morning.
It must have washed up here
with the early tide.
I fancy it would cover the lighthouse
if ever the need arose.
You must have been fucking whales
all night, judging by the distressed state
of the ocean and those three stranded
Leviathans still grunting happily.

Wonder what Lois would say if she heard of this?

A Cartoon History of The Spanish Civil War

MADRID: AFTER THE OPERA

This meticulous rioting,
this careful church burning
is certainly the work of Anarchists.
On our way from the Opera
we noticed two of them
casually disembowelling a priest
and then searching around
(rather forlornly I thought)
for a king.

SARAGOSSA: DEATH SQUAD

We were on our way to the cemetery
to dispose of another left-wing activist
(in retaliation for an earthquake in Ecuador)
when we spotted a gypsy near the gates
and decided to have a little fun.
We forced the red bastard to go over
and ask the gypsy to read his palm.
She told him the usual:
"You will be lucky in love,
marry well and have four children."
She was a little bemused
by our peals of laughter,
which were interrupted by four gunshots,
then continued louder than ever.

PROPAGANDA

"The Nationalists meantime sought to point out
the contrast between the 'hungry' Republic
and their own territory by an air-raid
of loaves of bread on Barcelona.
The Republicans replied with an air-raid
of shirts and socks to demonstrate
their alleged superiority in manufactured goods.
The Nationalists replied to this
with a bombardment of incendiaries
and high-explosives to reinforce the point
that the armament industries had fallen into their hands."
— Hugh Thomas

REVOLUTION: JULY 19TH

"One little fact illustrates it:
at one of my comrades houses in Barcelona,
the control patrol, after a routine inspection,
opened a bird-cage and liberated a canary
in the name of Revolutionary Spain."
— Manuel Casanova

DEATH AT DAWN: FUENTE GRANDE

"We've just killed Federico Garcia Lorca,
we left him in a ditch
and I fired two bullets into his arse
for being a queer."
— Juan Luis Trescastro

EPILOGUE: SIERRA NEVADA

Remember what it was in Winter
to squat around a fire
dreaming of a (popularly elected)
Popular Front victory in the Spring;
a heart-warming conflagration of Cathedrals
to welcome us back from the mountains
and the chance, that eagerly awaited chance,
to throw entire right-wing families
screaming down a mineshaft.

Note to An Autocrat

Have I mentioned Sulla?
supreme campaigner,
ruthless butcher (even you would be impressed),
vigorous reformer.
In 79 B.C.
he resigned his dictatorship,
dismissed his lictors
and walked home a private citizen:
absolute Imperial power
absolutely dismantling itself
and taking a quiet stroll into history.
You, on the other hand,
could drive to the airport
and fly to a comfortable exile in Washington
before I even begin
to finish this.

Lunch at The Yacht Club

Tucking into my lasagne and chips,
studying an illustrated article
in *Time* magazine concerning
the recent slaughter of Bengalis
in Assam which contains a photograph
of thirty-four children being laid
in neat rows to fit without difficulty
into a ready-made mass-grave,
I am reminded by the waiter
that I have yet to order dessert.
I cover the photograph
and ask for cheesecake.
With cream?
Certainly with cream!

Bedtime Story

Now, children,
let's all get snug under the duvet
and listen to Comrade Tek
of the Khmer Rouge.
He will demonstrate
with the aid of a live monkey
(which you may play with later)
how he used to kill
those nasty Lon Nol soldiers.
Watch carefully as he takes
a very sharp knife
and slits open the monkey's belly,
then, pressing along the sides of the cut
with the palms of his hands,
makes the liver pop out in one piece.
With a man, he says,
it would never be quite as easy:
more often than not,
in his experience,
he would have to use his foot
to exert the proper pressure
on the wound,
otherwise the liver
hardly ever came out completely.

Are you asleep?

Headgear of The Tribe

with apologies to Desmond O'Grady

Brits on the pavement,
ice in the wind,
my mother is knitting
my first balaclava.

Self-Portrait at 36

Head like a football,
heart like a barrel of thickening blood,
seventeen stones, irritable,
out of love.

Modern American Myths

Video Video

Charlton Heston seems to have cracked
an unintentional joke falling under
his chariot everyone in the Control Room
is laughing the S.W.A.T. Captain has dressed
in sports coat and slacks to promote a manual
on police humour a dead hostage persists
at the bottom of the screen as bystanders
wave to the camera the moon-ferry is
beaming down hedgerows theme-parks spanners
muesli Rembrandts trampolines vigilantes bird-baths
rolling-stock safety-valves roof-gardens traffic-lights
strait-jackets scrap-heaps the Sea of Japan.

Alive and Well

Bing Crosby is trying to make contact
through a slap-happy medium who keeps
getting Buddy Holly bursting into going down
in flames the Andrews Sisters are wombed-up
in Katmandu awaiting the record company's
call for instant rebirth (epiduralairportTopofthePops)
Roy Orbison is wink wink Second Secretary
at the Soviet Embassy in Kinshasa nod nod
working for the C.I.A. Jim Reeves is currently
a cheeseburger Fred Astaire a bucket of nails
Patsy Cline is really dead really missed.

"I'm dreaming of a wide krizzmass…"

DREAMTIME IN MACDONALDS

All Hell breaks loose as someone inadvertently opens the
Party Room door where thirty more Shirley Temple look-
alikes are being pampered crunched and minced to provide
tender tastier hamburgers the manager is cutting up rough
under persistent tabloid questioning concerning his third
sex-change operation the Vietnam Veteran is opening his
wrists lengthwise to the armpits the spree killer at the next
table has just lost count and decided to start again at murder
one the next person through the door in blue suede shoes
shit it's Evis!

NO REST FOR THE EXQUISITE

Scratch and sniff editions
on the soft-porn stands,
Marilyn Monroe
is being served up
with a hint of perspiration
in pursuit of the hundred millionth
hard-on.

Still Blue Rondo à la Turk

Probably rain later so what
can always stay in bed sink
deeper under the covers shut
out this dismal weather enjoy
(a quick wank?) a slow scan
across the steamy memory
of your utterlysexybody Jesus
I wish you were here right now
pressing your sweet weight down
and around the fierce throbbing length
of this massive erection.

Still Blue Rondo a la Turk
thumping away beneath loud
Summer rain still telling me
how this prince of mediocrity has
stolen your heart has changed
your life I would rather you
ran away with the entire Shia
Amal Militia one by one I would
rather go blind in one eye and shut
the other than see you settle
for this ordinary ordinary ordinary
pain in the arse.
I suppose I should really be glad
for you should wish you the best
of luck bollocks to that ~~Jack~~
                              Jill!

Don't suppose you might consider
spending the weekend I mean assuming
he's got to go to Manchester or Crewe or
somewhere and you really do feel pissed

off as the Princess of Regularity well you
know what I'm saying why not leave
a note in his pre-heated slippers and get
over here before I change the lock.

A Small Fit of Pique

Sitting up late again Fats Waller on the turn-
table scratched record much crackling but
getting through anyway I have managed to
transcend such minor details which would
probably annoy you intensely which gives
me a feeling of immense superiority which
makes it easier to dismiss these persistent
waves of longing or at least place them
in a proper perspective what are you doing
tonight you shit?

No I'm not angry not really angry weary
weary of carrying this small specially adapted
Buddhist temple on my shoulders and acting
with sweetness and light in the wake of your
defection with Doctor Schweitzer I feel like
letting rip occasionally and killing a few
menwomenandchildren strangling some
bayoneting others and setting the remainder
alight after soaking them in petrol but this
is merely a whim I would much rather
go to bed and curl up with a good assassin
and plan the disposal of your latest eternal
love bang bang bang.

I suppose that by now you have decided
that I have sold my soul am in league
with the devil actually she's just borrowed
it to make a detailed study in fact she
tells me she's writing a book.
Poems?
What fucking poems?

Dreams Apart

Tried to reach you on the dream-belt
last night too much interference though
became embroiled in a shampoo mystery
hedgehog world cup and couldn't lock on
to your warm radio image which was already
disrupting tea-time Jordanian T.V. needless
to say I woke in a lather of sweat mouthing
your lovely name into the pillow
Lavinia Lavinia Lavinia.

Then of course I actually saw you
patrolling a devastated Wellington Road
in Peoples' Liberation Army fatigues
forage cap pushed jauntily back on your
cropped dark hair cigarette clinging desperately
to your bored lower lip Kalashnikov slung
with casual menace from your left hip
much as I wanted to approach you I didn't dare
you were rumoured to be organizing
a women only arts council death-squad
from the remnants of the Korean trained
Second Armoured Brigade needless to say
I woke in a lather of sweat mouthing
your fearful name into the pillow
Pandora Pandora Pandora.

Turned out again swinging low over
the frantic neon towards the flat dark sea
plunged to the quiet beyond quiet depths
searching for your sweet history
in a split-open cream-coloured shell-like
mould needless to say I woke in a lather

of sweat mouthing your ancient name
into the pillow
Aphrodite Aphrodite Aphrodite.

Taking ten years off for good behaviour
or four and one half simple bacteriological
incarnations in Tierra Del Fuego would make
me a mere twenty three times I have tried
to tell you how lovely you are not laughing up your
sleeve is the slim beauty of your arm oh Aisling.

Long Valley Afloat

Head down in MacCurtain Street
against darkening weather step
into the light of your steady blue stare
blue light of the sky over Lima
blue level of the sea at Valparaiso
split-second later snow.

As I bleary crawling along the bar towards
oblivion met eye-level with the barman speaking
in tongues the long dreary scan of his life
without illumination love he imagined to be
like dropping a hand-grenade into a barrel
of hand-grenades Spring it was for I checked
with the Met Office twice.

I'm sorry I kissed your neck I meant to kiss
your navel but it was partially obscured by clouds
and anyway the weather forecast—I mean your hips
were already under water and apart from wading in
up to my waist and kneeling down I would not have been
able to kiss its exact centre which would have meant
upsetting the entire and extremely delicate balance
of the planet of course I was drunk I know that now
but at the time…

The bar a ship in a storm pitching
and rolling your dark hair framing
your suddenly underwater face your steady
blue stare centring a swirling universe
we swarm frantically against the mounting
amber waves across the frothy liquid uproar
your smile a lighthouse flashing welcome
and danger as we crash in a shoal
at your feet.

Poem on The Margin

That it should all
come down to this
obsessive hoarding
one body-length
hug three perhaps
four kisses (two
on the cheek) over Chris
tmas a friendly pat
on the head even
a handshake for
the New Year use
less useless I
wish I wish I
wish I was in
your arms
bugger it.

Ten Words in Irish
do Mháire Davitt

Í imithe
ar a Yamaha
go Omaha.

Mé buartha,
buartha,
buartha.

A Note on The Demise of Communism

I give the Communist salute
to my Capitalist ex-girlfriend
as she takes the corner at a clip
in her black BMW,
doles me out an imperious nod
and leaves me to choke back
Marxist-Leninist rhetoric
in a plume of carbon-monoxide.

Dark Tower   *Slow Metal Sea*

Just now you passed,
oblivious to my calm stare,
my unhurried heartbeat.
Even from the tower
it's easy to make out
the small disturbing swing
of your breasts,
the sudden alarming pout
of your vulva
through undulating denim.

I am in Crosshaven,
the wind is even further out
harassing the Azores.
Thinking of you,
I begin to imagine
the slow honeyed burn of your skin
against the slow honeyed burn of mine.
All this time you are in Midleton,
so much for foreplay.

Later it happens:
I am standing at the bar
quietly supping
when you pass so close
you hook your left breast
into the crook of my elbow
making me snort
into my pint.

Slipping out of my jackboots
so as not to disturb the budgerigar,
I creep softly past the leopard's cage

66

only to confront
your wide-eyed,
owl-awake mother.

So, I am waiting
at the bottom of the cliff path,
directly below the tower,
for the moon to come out
and set the slow metal sea
bristling with silver.
Afterwards I will climb up alone;
already my tongue
is working urgently
against the roof of my mouth,
perfecting those wet flickering circles
around your nipples.

Little Island Reverie
for Tom McCarthy

Day-dreaming here
where the Lee sweeps 'round
Blackrock Castle and surges
across the sullen mud-flats
towards a calm preoccupied sea.
Shore birds wheel and flash,
skimming the brightening waters
in precise, split-second formations,
their small piping cries
exquisitely desolate.
A freighter throbs upriver,
navigation lights feeble
in the afternoon glare,
Tuan Jim, in silhouette,
brooding on the prow.

My Dead Father Reading Over My Shoulder

Madrid. Late November.
Mid-morning on the Plaza Cibeles
under a newly-installed, blue-tinted,
plate-glass sky.
Coffee, croissants and the Herald Tribune,
simple empire of the moment.
The café's one-eyed cat
calm among the pigeons
as frantic shoals of traffic
anxiously negotiate the Square.

Light on the Paseo del Prado,
light on the page
as I drowsily scan a report
on the World Series:
"first base", "pinch hit", "home run",
phrases floating out past my ken
as if being read by someone else.

Buy your own paper, father.

My Mother Alive and Well and Living in…

Six months after
the report of your death,
I start a rumour among my schoolmates
that you are still alive.
That you are hiding out
in the Bolivian Andes
with a Lt. Colonel of the Treasury Brigade
who fled La Paz during one of three
October coups d'état
with thirty million U.S. dollars
and four lorry-loads of gold.

Just wait for the letters,
I tell them,
and the postal-orders.

Epitaph for an Old I.R.A. Man

That gas-pipe baluba, my grandfather,
has blown his last dart
into the stratosphere.
We found him grinning
under the wheels of the Royal Carriage
this morning,
his un-exploded corgi-bomb
pressed to a jelly.

Post-Colonial Awakening
for Mick Hannigan

Pith-helmeted little imperialists,
snug in the school cinema,
we watched
that pompous colonial epic:
Sanders of the River.
We shouldered the White Man's Burden,
gravely resolved to improve
the savage African's savage lot,
until the projectionist, Brother Keating,
ran the entire film again in reverse,
dissolving our grim determination
in tears of laughter.

Memories of Old Moscow
for Paul Durcan

Spring it is,
daffodils
and leaping squirrels
in leafing trees,
the Politburo winding up
to speak
of Lenin.

White Nights on Douglas Street

KIND OF BLUE

Not that it means anything,
that kiss,
it was tucked away
in the steaming archives of desire
even before I turned back
into the room to exhume
the long dead party.
Not that it means anything,
the hiss of your bicycle tyres
on the wet tarmac
echoing through my head
long after you turned down
the hill and well into
Ian Dury's thumping rendition of
Wake Up and Make Love with Me.

A COUPLE OF NIGHTS LATER

A couple of nights later
I am turning over
into another dream wilderness
when a tiny residue of your scent,
trapped in some hitherto undisturbed pore,
is released into the still air of the bedroom,
greening the wilderness.

THE PLEASURES OF CELIBACY

On Capwell Road this Summer,
the back gate to the church
is firmly locked.
They must have gotten wind
of those Winter evenings
we spent in meltdown
against the presbytery wall,
while, in the bedroom above,
caught up in the pant
of our endless foreplay,
the young curate prayed feverishly,
his vows creaking and groaning.

THE DEEPEST MIRTH

That you may always be thus, without torment
and seldom, if ever, count sheep.
Articulating the gift of the moment:
a lovely woman laughing in her sleep.

SUMMER NIGHTS SOUTH CHANNEL

On Parliament Bridge
we would talk and talk
over the churning roar of water,
the occasional sigh of traffic.
Until the tide turned,
swelling darkly in the channel,
kissing up under the arch,
making the weir shut up.

DREAM TALK

"Too much salami,"
you whisper,
turning into my arms.
"Beware of frog swallowers,"
I reply
my tongue sliding down
to arouse
your drowsy clitoris.

GOOD NIGHT LOUIS STEWART

Not thinking of you, not exactly,
down by the river actually,
adding a steaming golden trickle
to its steady brown flow.
Any minute now
you will probably roar past here
hotly pursued by the Harbour Police.
Not thinking of you, not at all,
sitting at the window actually,
entering the microcosm
by staring hard at an orange.
Any minute now
you are going to emerge
through a rip in the tablecloth
momentarily serene.
Not thinking of you, not anymore,
laid back on the bed actually,
listening to Louis Stewart's liquid guitar
floating up from the kitchen.
Any minute now he's going to play
There Will Never Be Another You.

32 Fish

for Nessa

Night settles in
along the river.
Moonlight scans
the calm blue-black flood
from bank to silvered bank.
A swan turns majestically
like a screwdriver.

Existential Café
for Tony O'Connor

"Essence before existence!"
declared the waitress,
throwing a handful of flour
and a few raisins
onto the table.

"I ordered two scones,"
said Jean-Paul.

Café Paradiso

Grim armies marching
in the rumbling pit
of my stomach
as I wait among
the staring, sniggering tables
until all complaints
at your increasing
lateness are lost
in a sudden blur of kisses
with the waitress.

Warm Air Front
for Katherine

STOPPING THE PLANET IN ST. LUKE'S

I have just come to rest
in Fruit and Vegetables
after a dizzy whirl
through Sweets and Biscuits
when you arrive in the shop,
trailing bright fragrant weather,
flashing that bone-melting grin.

The Earth is momentarily still,
then resumes its slow majestic spin.

BREATHLESS IN THE HIBERNIAN BAR

A tongue of flame
licks into place
above your head
as you begin to speak
and I am suddenly afloat
in the upper air
of an overwhelming inspiration.

Far below
in the absolute stillness of the bar,
your one good lung
breathes for us both.

DROWNING ON WELLINGTON ROAD

Not so much
singing in the rain
as charmed out of its dismal reach
by that kiss at the corner
just moments ago.
It may have put a significant dent
in that sullen mass of liquid
swirling in from the coast.

No matter,
I was already underwater
and your kiss simply snatched
that last gasp of air
I was carefully saving for it.

Kissing Maura O' Keeffe

You know thursdays and me
warp nine through the gamma quadrant
to flush dead pigeons from the shuttle-bay
a slow swing around orion to collect
my twenty-nine senses early morning banter
with the milkman the paper boy the post
person farsud zwingli vabblesap beam
down to the uptown grill suck on
burger chips beans sausages mushrooms
and onions tilt full fat face towards
that rare shaft of sunlight glinting off
a wing-mirror dream of holding mary mahony
squeezing niamh connolly kissing maura
o' keeffe somewhere over the rainbow
somewhere over the rainbow my bollocks.

I can't remember what I was looking at
so intently that particular day probably
the cracks in the pavement or those cute
smears of dog-shit which I am convinced
will eventually conform to some quasi-
mystical pattern I have already laid down
in my subconscious and lead to momentary
if ultimately meaningless revelation but
that's another story however I was aware
of that black scarf floating in and out
of my peripheral vision like a remnant
of the last anarchist banner from the last
burning barricade but then I started looking
at you I mean really looking at you head
up straight between those beautiful blue
eyes only to see the enormous sullen
bulk of myself looking back in grim stereo.

So scrap entire physical dimension
all change year zero back to the future
blueprints under your pillow with assorted
limbs life-support system not to be switched
on until a wave and then another breaking
gently at your feet a scarf wound lightly
about your neck or the hallstand's this
friendship developing still without simple
nourishment will probably lose weight no
problem I can go without holding you easy
don't need so much as want can always hold
myself kiss kiss want to see you though
whatever the arrangement holograms and
tapes if you like hello?

Bang

after Greg Delanty

Finally sold out,
exhausted but happy,
the balloon seller
leans for a breather
on the roof
of the car-bomb.

What?

I am up close to the radio,
listening late and at low volume
to the World Service
when the house shudders.
My brother is tumbling purposefully
down the stairs.
Eighteen stones of spluttering indignation
in a tiny red underpants,
bearing a message from his wife:
"Would you ever go to bed,
you're keeping the canary awake…"

Letters to Michaela

Dearest M,
I am waiting up tonight
until the city quietens,
the sea stills
and the freaks calm down.
Until the Swedish North Atlantic Fleet
squeezes eagerly out of the Baltic
and I can hear all the way from Malmö,
the sound of your even-breathing,
untroubled sleep.
I would send
a kiss to your eyelids,
a kiss to your nipples,
a kiss to your lips
but just now
you are probably spending
your Social Security money
on ice-cream in Greece.

If it was raining—
a sudden downpour
which made the Square swim,
the taxis dive for cover,
the very statues
gasp for breath—
the sound
would invariably drown out
the sound of your bare feet
on the stairs,
if you were here.

There are waterholes in the Sudan
which would be big enough
to take both of us,

which would enable us to spend
the long hot afternoons
immersed and undressing,
which would inevitably
bring us closer together,
your eyes reflecting
smooth green desert,
your breasts finding perfect level
against my chin.

Nothing to report really:
a hint of Summer
wafting up from the waterfront,
two oranges glowing
on the bedside table,
muted traffic noise,
dreary racket-ball,
dust, fumes, the smell of *Bergasol.*
Nightly, under a gleaming indifferent moon,
the hushed coast of the Levant
yearns for you,
especially Jaffa,
whose lights through the window,
beyond the abyss at the bottom of the bed,
wink longingly.

The Empty Quarter

Where you are tonight
or what you are doing
is immaterial.
In this
your tent is already pitched
at a cool caravanserai
under creaking date-palms.
Your camels are watered, fed, rested
and reciting the secret names of Allah.
You are reclining
in black diaphanous silks
on a jewel-encrusted divan,
where I (in Richard Gere's body)
am kissing you
into a long hot shivering fit.

Pure Naked Idyll

Before the after-play,
the heart lies charmed,
the head forgets politics
snug between the drowsy lift
of your breasts as if
nothing in the World
could stir
breathe
sink
swim
spin.

Keeping in Shape
for Liam O' Callaghan

"Room for two more?"
I wheeze at the gravedigger
as we jog heavily
past the graveyard.

"Two and more,"
he replies,
loudly, heartily, eternally.

An Idiot's Guide to the American Civil War
for Val Bogan

FORT SUMTER BEGINS TO FESTER

On the evening of December 26th 1860
Major Robert Anderson
moved his command,
with admirable stealth and skill,
from Fort Moultrie to Fort Sumter,
thereby destroying an understanding
between the seceding States and Washington.

Did this "one true man" make war inevitable?

SENATOR CHESTNUT BOASTS

In February 1861
at a Gala Ball in Richmond,
in an effort to impress his listeners,
Senator James Chestnut offers to drink
all the blood spilt over the issue of secession.

In April 1974,
up to his waist
in the bright arterial flow of Second Manassas,
his champagne glass stained and brittle
with constant use,
he belches blood in the face
of an over-inquisitive history student
from Tokyo.

The Birth of 'Stonewall' Jackson

On Henry House Hill,
after fighting through the morning,
the Confederates began falling back at noon
just as Jackson brought his fresh troops
into line behind the crest.
General Bee, trying to rally his broken brigade,
pointed at Jackson's men and shouted:
"There's Jackson standing like a stone wall,
rally behind the Virginians!"

or did he?
some observers claim Bee's remarks
were uttered in exasperation:
"Look at Jackson standing there
like a damned stone wall!"

Shiloh Hits An Artery

The twenty thousand casualties
at Shiloh
were nearly double the number
of casualties at First Manassas,
Wilson's Creek, Fort Donelson and Pea Ridge

combined.

Antietam Goes With The Flow

More than twice as many Americans
lost their lives in one day of battle
at Antietam as fell in combat
in the War of 1812, the Mexican War
and the Spanish American War

combined.

Marye's Heights: The Dead Burying the Dead

"They sprawled in every conceivable position,
some on their backs with gaping jaws,
some with eyes as large as walnuts,
protruding with glassy stares,
some doubled up like contortionists.
Here lay one without a head,
there one without legs,
yonder a head and legs
without a trunk;
everywhere horrible expressions,
fear, rage, agony, madness, torture;
lying in pools of blood, lying with heads
half buried in mud, with fragments of shell
sticking in oozing brains,
with bullet holes all over their puffed limbs."

On the Eve of Chancellorsville Jackson Dips into the Continuum

Stuart has just informed
General Lee and me
that Hooker's right flank
is "in the air" three miles west of Chancellorsville.
If we can plot a route
through the "wilderness" tonight
we will teach "those people"
another hard lesson tomorrow.
Keep hearing Frank Sinatra
singing *Old Devil Moon*
over and over in my head.

Who is Frank Sinatra?

Grant Takes The Arithmetic

All that Summer
From Spotsylvania through Cold Harbour
to Petersburg
the butcher's bill comes due.
Wave upon wave
breasting the earthworks
and breaking in blood
on the Confederacy's prolonged death-throes.
Grant wades on grimly towards Richmond.

"I am in blood stepped in so deep…"

Lincoln Gets His

A half-muffled explosion,
bluish smoke in the Presidential Box.
"Sic Semper Tyrannis!"
or "Revenge for the South!"
or "The South shall be free!"

whatever,
Lincoln sits sprawled
in his rocker
as if asleep.

Davis Becomes President

After two years in Fort Munroe,
shackled and abused,
Davis was released on bail.
He spent some months in Europe
as persistent attempts were made
to bring him to trial, conviction
and a "sour apple tree".
Returning to the United States
late in 1869,
with all legal proceedings
against him quashed,
he accepted the position of President
of The Carolina Life Insurance Company.

Self-Portrait at 33

Quick scan of the horizon
this "year of miracles"
reveals smouldering ruins
gradually reducing to ash,
a couple of lepers complaining
to the Department of Social Welfare
and the Department of Health,
Lazarus still cold, still flat;
nothing to get nailed up about, yet.

For Peace Comes Dropping Slow

after W.B. Yeats

A girl passes
on the footpath,
a girl
with a lovely brown speck
in one of her blue blue eyes
and you think
the World will probably end
sweetly after all,
or at least
that the Bomb
will drop softly
like a Cathedral.

Fortune

after Luis De Gongora

Fortune presents gifts
according to her whims,
not according to the book.
She blinds the prophet in one eye
and gives the village idiot second sight.
When you expect whistles, it's flutes,
when flutes, whistles.

Her circuitous routes cannot be traced
as she distributes honours and millstones.
To the altar boy
she grants riches without precedent,
while plunging the Archbishop
headlong into penury.
When you expect whistles, it's flutes,
when flutes, whistles.

Because a pauper has stolen an egg
he swings from the gallows,
while the Governor short-changes
the hangman once again.
When you expect whistles, it's flutes,
when flutes, whistles.

End of Part One

Dead to the earth dead to the faint wriggle
of Spring through the slagheaps until somehow
a new muse sparks in the familiar gloom
like a faulty cigarette lighter I switch on
the sweet flicker of desire again wind up
the slack coil of lust to singing tightness
begin dreaming of your wet 7% yellow
stock-market crashes on derelict lighthouse
news and here's

John Fitzgerald Kennedy almost within arm's
reach definitely within range standing up
in an open-top Cadillac waving frantically
at me and shouting SHOOT YOU FOOL
SHOOT it's June '63 on Military Hill
I'm ten years of age unarmed except
for a congealed wad of liquorice in my
pocket and anyway my mother is right
beside me squeezing my trigger-finger
much too tightly in her excitement.

Onwards and upwards you declared
nudging me towards the pit and the long
drop into unutterable stillness—
when I crawled out it was to John Coltrane
faint but soothing in the distance the agitated
shuffling of my own feet and the weary
dole operative still patiently explaining
the revised butter allowance: "listen earthling..."

Intimations of Mortality

Not long after
the Tooth Fairy stopped
leaving shiny new pennies
under my pillow,
the Angel of Death,
gathering my mother
into his huge beating wings,
shook a dusty black feather
onto my bed.

Breakthrough

Mexico, 1970.
World Cup, quarter final.
England, two up against West Germany
and cruising.
My brother, quietly gloating,
my father and I plunged
into glum, staring silence.
I go out into the kitchen
to make tea,
West Germany claw one back.
"Too little, too late,"
my brother declares.
I go back into the kitchen,
West Germany equalize.
My father and I are led out,
blinking, into the daylight.

In extra-time,
Müller, 'Der Bomber', scores the winner.
I had never hugged my father,
I haven't hugged him since.

Noli Me Tangere

Just a glance will do
a kiss would be much too much
the weight of your lips.

So It Goes

You know how it happens:
The woman you have been
so eager to meet for so long
is standing in front of you,
listening, quite intently,
to your somewhat excited babble
when the tiniest fleck of spittle
exits the side of your mouth,
describes a lovely slow parabola
through the astonished air
and lands plumb on her cheek.
To her eternal credit
she doesn't flinch, even in the slightest
and waits until you are out of sight
before reaching for her handkerchief.

The Ferbane Haiku

Long live nothingness
beyond this puny heart-song
this wretched wheezing.

Bite your whining tongue
the loveliest woman here
is looking at you.

Cancel the doctor
this naked conversation
is healing enough.

Up Yours Gay Byrne

Look on the bright side you can always
blow your brains out during the next
whiter than white detergent commercial
you can turn it down or even turn it off
and storm out into the hallway and stamp
on the landmine you were saving
for the T.V. licence inspector look
on the bright side you could be the third
literary critic this week being beaten
prior to being necklaced you could be
lying on any street in any major town
with three bullet wounds in the head
after swearing under your breath
in Danish at a Conradh na Gaeilge
roadblock look on the bright side
any day now during the next ten million
years the sun is due to expand
to seventy times its present size
before dwindling to the dimensions
of an orange we may have already
returned to the Crab Nebula by then
in the form of a super-intelligent vapour
it's Urbi et Orbi next after this word
from our sponsors.

Bathroom Vignette

The hot tap
is speaking out of the corner
of its mouth:
"Twenty years steaming service
and for what? For what?"

The cold tap
remains silent, disdainful.

The plughole is all ear.

Labyrinth

I'm relying on reflections here:
the reception area,
a little like Plato's cave,
each successive glass-panelled door
carrying an image of the sunlit garden,
reversed, corrected, reversed again;
shifted right, left, right and finally left
onto the steeply angled window-panes
and into the bewildered lens
of the surveillance camera
above the bevelled security mirror.
When you came in, just then,
with your silly questions
and your supercilious grin,
I was rendered speechless
by the grotesque solidity
of your presence.

A Mantra for Niamh Connolly

The heron's stillness
against the stark raving weir's
incessant babbling.

Off Summerhill South

MIDSUMMER VIGNETTE

An afternoon breeze
is lifting the curtains
along Douglas Street.
Its huge elemental breathing
fills the room,
cooling our drowsy after-play.
We lie where we fell,
tangled in half-discarded underwear,
levelled by ecstasy.

BALACLAVA

I am perched
on the edge of the bed,
naked except for a pair
of black lace panties
drawn down over my face
in order to inhale
your still warm, still moist smell,
again
and again
and again.

REDUCTIONIST LOVE POEM

Never again
your lovely face in mine
as I wake and blah, blah, blah.
Never again
my arms around you

as I sleep, etcetera, etcetera.
Never again
the rising heat, the cooling passion
and so on.
Never again
those long involved conversations
after midnight
but then, never before.

After Goethe

All nine of them—
the Muses of course—
used to visit me.
I ignored them
for the warmth of your arms,
the sweetness of your kisses.
Then you left me
and they vanished.
I looked about
for a knife or a rope,
anything lethal and to hand
but I was saved by boredom.
Boredom, Mother of the Muses.

Under the Dog Star

Imminent synchronicity wakes me.
I open my eyes as the digital clock
displays 3.33.33 a.m.
Beyond the window
a gleaming curve holds up
the dark weight of the moon.
Further out fierce starlight
glitters through from 1347.
Even the dogs are silent—
shot, knifed and bludgeoned into silence.
Thinking of you,
I begin to imagine you
slipping out of the satin hush
of your underwear
into the chafing din of my arms.
Trouble is, you are probably awake also,
busy in the sealed-off archives of memory
shredding this fiction.

Finally I admit to myself
that you will not call
and apart from burning offerings
next to the silent phone,
apart from racking the postman
until he snaps and coughs up
all those letters you insist you sent,
I can do nothing.
So, I sit in the gloom
unravelling steadily,
the gleam of a demented smile
growing brighter and brighter
as I disassemble the rose—
shelovedmeshelovedmenotshelovedmeshe—
reassemble the machine-pistol.

This is where I peel your name
from that battered, much-travelled suitcase—
the heart.
Where I dissolve whole reels of memories
which played and played
in that obsessive, all-hours cinema—
the head.
This is where
I switch off the individually-lit photographs
and burn down the dreary warehouse of regret.
Where I walk out
into the sweet empty air,
into the desert of myself.

Last Night

after Müller

As I passed,
I wrote: "Who but me?"
reversed in the frost on your window
under the effervescent stars.

In The Beginning

God falls apart,
awareness glitters in the burnished deserts of obsidian,
an astonished sky contemplates an astonished ocean.

Extracts from *The Lost Log-Book* *of Christopher Columbus*

for John Montague

FRIDAY AUGUST 3rd 1492

We set out from the bar of Saltes
and travelled with a strong breeze sixty miles,
that is to say fifteen leagues, Southward
before sunset. Afterwards we changed course
to South-West by South, making for the Canaries.

MONDAY AUGUST 6th 1492

The rudder of the Pinta, whose Captain
is Martin Alonso Pinzón, jumped out of position.
This is said to be the doing of Gomez Rascón
and Cristóbal Quintero, the owner of the Pinta,
who dislike the voyage.

THURSDAY SEPTEMBER 6th 1492

We set out this morning to continue our voyage
after nearly a month spent in the Canaries
repairing the Pinta.

FRIDAY SEPTEMBER 7th

All day becalmed.

SUNDAY SEPTEMBER 9th

We made fifteen leagues today
but I decided to score up a smaller amount
so as not to alarm the crew who might
take fright at a long voyage.

MONDAY SEPTEMBER 10TH

Sixty leagues this day and night.
Scored up forty eight.

FRIDAY SEPTEMBER 14th

The crew of the Niña say they have seen
a tern and a tropic bird, neither of which
go more than twenty five leagues from land.

SATURDAY SEPTEMBER 15th

Early this evening we saw a marvellous
streak of fire fall into the sea
about four leagues from the ships.

SUN. SEPT. 16th

The weather is like April in Andalusia.

THURS. 20th

Two boobies flew to the Santa Maria
and we saw much weed, a sure sign of land.

SUN. 23rd

All day becalmed.
The crew grumbled, saying there would be no wind
to carry them back to Spain.

TUE. 25th

At sunset Martin Alonso went up
into the poop of the Pinta
and called out most joyfully
that he could see land.
I fell on my knees and gave thanks to God.

WED. 26th

What we had taken for land was a cloud bank.

THURSDAY 27th

We saw a tropic bird.

SAT. 29Th

Two boobies.

TUESDAY OCTOBER 2nd

A gull.

WED. 3rd

Petrels.

THURS. 4th

A frigate bird came to the ship.

FRIDAY 5th

Many flying fish.

TUESDAY 9th

All night we heard birds passing.

FRIDAY 12th

We sighted land some two leagues away,
some naked people appeared.

SATURDAY 13th

A petrel and a frigate.

SUNDAY 14th

A booby and a tern.

WEDNESDAY 24th

More weed.

Oedipus in Harlem

Yo! Muthafucker

Among Thieves

for Michael O'Riordan

"There are pickpockets in the Cathedral,"
warned the bishop.
"They may get to your purses before we do,"
muttered the worried priest.

Exit

after the Irish, 9th century

With an eye on Heaven,
the blind girl
has thrown herself
into the well.

There is a God

after Rimbaud

There is a God,
Who beams at the damask altar-cloths;
Who basks in the golden glow of the chalices;
Who dozes to the lullaby of Hosannas.
When grieving mothers
come to the church for solace
and let their pennies
rattle into the big iron box,
He wakes up disgruntled
and fires down a dose of clap
at the priest.

Too Lovely for Words

for Edel

Strange to say
I was elbow-deep in the dictionary
when you called.
Looking up the precise meaning
of "exquisite".
"Your exquisite face etcetera, etcetera..."
"Stunned into heart-troubled silence
by your exquisite, whatever..."
And then, of course,
your brush-fire hair
your eyes of needles and candles
your ears of tremors and rumours
your nose of lemon and cardamom
your mouth of honey and infamy
your tongue of nightmare and ravings
your voice of sudden tumultuous
announcements in the wilderness
your neck of birch and whispers
your throat of shuddering guitars
your shoulders of feathers and tendons
your back of ebony and lamentations
your arms of spanners and cables
your hands of paper and thunder
your fingers of salmon and destiny
your breasts of apples and planets
your belly of wheat and lightning
your buttocks of pure gold
your thighs of hammers and demons
your vulva of crevice and cleft
of fern-shaded rock-pools deep in the forest
of burning afternoons
your legs of seraph and antelope

126

your ankles of poise and desire
your feet of distance and dreaming
your exquisite toes.

The Big Issues

Word comes through
that you are working your ass off.
If there is one as lovely
in the teeming seraglio
of a Turkish soccer player,
I'll eat my fez.
If there are breasts more shapely
beneath the vests
of Mao's fearless militia women,
I'll swallow my little red book.

Niamh in Doheny & Nesbitt's

When you came into the bar
that Sunday afternoon,
the entire clientele
tilted precariously on their stools
to steal a glimpse
of your spell-binding beauty.
When you reached across the counter
to collect your pint and crisps,
creaking in those poured-into denims,
the famous stopped clock shuddered
and began to click again.

Welcome to oblivion.

Bells' Field Haiku

for Sarah Durcan

A housefly sunbathes
on the glossy veranda
of an ivy leaf.

A sullen cloud mass
drags grey underskirts of rain
along the river.

A belfry starts up—
a sweet iron clamouring
swells from the city.

Oh Fuck Off

No mention in the Morning Clarion
of the miraculous appearance of the image
of an image of the Blessed Virgin in raised pastry
on a chicken and mushroom pie in a fish and
chip shop on the South Douglas Road or of the vast
and already heaving multitudes quickly bussed into
place and intoning decade after decade of the rosary
or of the swivelling dick-head dead Elvis look-alike
who purchased the marvellous pie and insisted
upon his inalienable right to consume it there and
then much to the chagrin of the murmuring throng.

And yes you do get tired of it all the entire
or at least the observable Universe and the
aloof orbital indifference of the planets and the
grotesque distances between stars and the eternal
oscillation between expansion and contraction
and the growing realization that everything
you have said and done up to now with the
understandable exception of an evening alone
in the paradisal shadows of the Alhambra
may be part of an extremely elaborate dream
you are having in your tipsy mother's womb
or the awful possibility that you are already
a thousand years dead and haunting the shattered
empty shell of your self and the grim probability
that it would have been infinitely better for
all concerned if you had never been born
in fact it would solve everything for once
and for all if someone could arrange
to send that little Dutch fucker back through
a worm-hole in the space-time continuum
to stick his finger in the Big Bang.

This is the fourth time I have met that
endoftheworldisnigher idiot the day after
his predicted end of the world whimper
and this is the fourth time he has justified
the ultimate non-event with the pompous
declaration that to all intents and purposes
the world ended ages ago with the awareness
of the interminable recycling of History and
the whirling momentum of Time and just
as I am beginning to think that he is right
after all I read in the Evening Bugle
that this very same prick-in-the-furze
has won the Lotto I mean even to do the Lotto...

Portents Portents

A good omen,
the robin coming into view,
is trying to overtake
a bad omen,
the crow disappearing from sight.
My mother croaks,
clutching her lottery ticket.

Melville Terrace

for Hugh

Who knows?
A hundred years from now
I may still be here.
A swallow flitting in and out
through warping roof-beams
or a rat scrambling across
a jumble of worm-eaten books,
unremittingly cheerful.

Dispersal

When I am finally burned to a crisp,
pounded to a fine ash by steam-hammers
and scattered from South-facing cliffs
over a disconsolate sea,
I would hope
that at least one fundamental particle
of my being could occasionally recycle
to the sunlit shallows below Myrtleville,
there to swirl playfully
around your thousand-year-old feet.

Haiku for Norman McCaig

The bittern's lament
recalling the giddy soul
to its loneliness.

Paseo

i.m. Federico Garcia Lorca

I almost envy you
that pre-dawn stroll beyond Viznar.
The firing squad, eagerly preparing
to rid Holy Spain of four more reds,
is taking careful aim at your backs.
An early morning breeze
is making mischief among the pines.
I can imagine
that half-terrified, half-fascinated
look over your shoulder
as you wonder
if the old adage holds true:
that you will not hear the bullet
that kills you.
The headlights of the trucks
keep you targeted
until the fusillade crashes out,
calling a halt to your final paseo.

Self-Portrait at 46

There is my penis,
gathering fluff
beneath the soft horizon
of my underpants.

Ballynoe Haiku

My kisses like bees
in your honey-coloured hair
sweetly mistaken.

Your kisses like rain
on the forgotten desert
of my abdomen.

Honey

There's none can tell
how much I missed
your pouting, bee-stung lips,
which look as if
you kept your mouth
hard-pressed against
a hive's busy entrance
all Summer long.

Long Summer Afternoon
for Gráinne

As you sleep,
your tanned pelt
glowing against lemon sheets,
a warm southern wind
whips a sprinkling of rain
through the open window:
A blind cartographer
mapping you with kisses.

In the name of memory,
I claim that quicksilver
trickle of sweat;
its sinuous track
down into the small
of your back;
its slight tickling
at the top
of your buttocks;
its happy drip
into fragrant darkness.

Three days,
two showers later,
your smell fades
from my skin
and I submerge without trace
in the grubby quotidian.
Then, one morning,
several weeks after,
I pull on my grey sweater—
the very one you pressed
into service as a nightgown—
and suddenly inhale you
all over again.

Water Myth

for Patricia

"Whatever inspires,"
you call from the shower,
the water stunned into droplets
on your suddenly delicious skin.
"Well," I reply,
from the airport
twenty-seven years later,
"even with arms,
in your presence
the Venus de Milo
would be queuing
to be kissed."

The O'Neill Suite

WOOD SPRITE

In the afternoon quiet
of the café,
in the green-gold light
of your company,
a light flickering down
through dense canopies of leaves
to glimmer on the forest floor
of your deeply untroubled mind.

CAHERLAG

It was late
and I wanted to talk quietly
to your heart
but the wind
was chasing its tail
through the trees along the avenue,
the rain was trying out
a new syncopation
on the bins in the yard
and a sudden tumult of voices
in my head drowned out
your disconcerting aria.

BEMUSED

This morning,
your voice on the radio;
your face at the bottom
of the cereal bowl

I have been trying to fill;
your smile in the glint
on the handle of the tea cup;
your neck in the fluted stem
of the juice-stained glass
I have been twisting and twisting.

BALANCING ACT

I have been trying
to forget you,
in eight other arms,
seven legs.
But it's useless,
even the one-legged beauty
topples into insignificance
at the rising thought of you.

RELATIVE DENSITIES

If I have fallen for you,
it has been
with the improbable weight
of a feather;
the burrowing impudicity
of the flea;
the charm and spin
of a still undiscovered
fundamental particle.

BIRDSONG

I have been dreaming
in the solitary tree of your head,
beneath the wet black leaves
of your hair,
of the shining opal
of your breasts.

BE FRUITFUL AND MULTIPLY

I would like to hang
over your lovely dark head
like a sweetly dipping branch
of your favourite apple tree, just once.
I would like to pop you,
in your denim jacket
into a cloning booth,
sending copies
back throughout the ages.

Rain

Say we went out anyway
under a steady hissing of rain;
say we took the crumbling path
back across the cliffs
above the booming cove;
say we kissed in the periodic glare
from the lighthouse;
say we climbed the ninety-seven steps
to the top of the tower,
undressing as we climbed
and tumbled wet and breathless
onto your welcoming bed;
say you invited me to read
the astonishing astrological predictions
you had had tattooed
on your eloquent skin;
say I am reading still.

Ode 32

after Catullus

Give me a call this afternoon
if you have nothing else on,
especially clothes.
We could make love
into the evening and beyond.
Leave the back door off the latch,
tie up that snarling mastiff,
don't change your mind
and go shopping.
Get ready in your room
to come at least nine times
in quick succession,
just for starters.
In fact, I can come over right now.
I'm just lounging on the sofa,
stroking myself,
wondering what to do next
with this twitching erection.

Woof Woof

after Goethe

Of all the noises that irritate me—
car-alarms, Mormons, Cage's *4'33"*—
there's nothing as infuriating
as dogs barking late at night.
My sensitive ears are outraged
by their incessant howling.
Though, there is one mangy cur
whose occasional yelp
fills me with delicious anticipation,
since he once barked
at your unexpected arrival.
Now, when I hear him,
I think you might be coming,
or, better still, I remember a time
I waited for you and you came.

Rush Hour

I know the pedestrian light
is in your favour
and you must go and go now
but I want to linger
just a little longer in your embrace
at the corner of Washington Street
and South Main Street.
I want to kiss
each individual hair of your head
from root to tip
while the lights change and change again
and the city grinds to a shuddering halt
and the sky tilts over
to reveal teeming constellations,
utterly silent, unbearably distant.

Further Out

I can't tell you
where this is happening.
I know it's a dream
because the left bank of the Seine
has just appeared directly opposite
the right bank of the Lee.
I know it's daylight,
or at least dream daylight,
that silver-grey, residual glow
from some imploding star
shining in your glossy black hair.
I know it's you
because there is not one
even remotely as beautiful
on the stony inner planets
and I know you have been kissing me
for over a minute
because I have just woken up
gasping for breath.

Long Valley Revisited

Middle age is whispering on Winthrop Street:
"a taxi, a cup of cocoa and then to bed."
A full moon over Marlboro Street
is exhorting me to stay out,
perk up, think nineteen, get a life!
Trees are stretching into leaf
along the South Mall,
planets are flying wildly past
their preordained perihelia,
bats are fucking frantically in the belfries.
So, I am curling up my toes,
I am sloughing off this ageing skin,
I am kissing Mary Mahony.

Whatever Happened to Patsy Corbett?

That was the Summer
the face of the unattainable Marie Flynn
was joined in the crammed pantheon of lust
by the quickly-tanning limbs of Patsy Corbett.
When the boys of Mount Farran
tossed-off into their socks
through the hot July nights,
dreaming of a first wet kiss
from those lips of a palpable heaven.
That student riotous Summer of '68,
or was it '67?

Seán Guevara Lynch

When you heard
of Che's execution in Higueras in '67,
did you allow yourself
a little tug of regret,
if only for a long lost kinsman?
Not to mention
a hint of admiration
for his devotion to action,
if not even envy
for his abrupt dispatch?
"There, but for six All Ireland medals
and the millstone of Cork around my neck,
goes Commandante Jack."

Clean Exit

A good day to die
the laundry basket empty
fresh linen to hand.

Escape

after Katarzyna Borun

We set up camp
beside the motorway,
outside the halting-site.
The last Hiace van
parked behind bullet-proof glass
in the Museum.
Around us, beyond the reach
of calloused hands,
the city howled on its leash.

Ablutions

after Mandelstam

I was washing at night in the courtyard,
stars glittered serenely overhead.
Starlight like salt sprinkled on an eyeball,
the rain-butt full and freezing over.

The gates slammed and secured
and the earth truly desolate.
Nothing more pure, more bitter
than truth's empty canvas.

A star melts like sugar in the barrel
and the freezing water seems suddenly deeper.
Death cleaner, misfortune sweeter
and the world more truthful, more terrible.

Pushkin's Moment

for Síabhra

July 1st 1832. Peterhof, Empress's Birthday.
The Imperial Family and Court
offer themselves, in their full majesty,
to the public gaze.
Resplendent in a long line of opulent lineiki,
they are moving slowly
through a dense throng of awed peasants
when Pushkin, hurrying along
by the side of the road,
is spotted and hailed by the Tsar:
"Bonjour Pouchkine!"
"Bonjour Sire," he replies,
without breaking his stride.

Fame

after Arrian

Having concluded the formalities
of an alliance with the Celtic tribes
from the Adriatic coast,
Alexander indulges in a little friendly banter.
What, he asks them,
do they fear most in the world,
thinking they must answer,
if only out of politeness,
"You, O Great Lord!"
They reply
that they live in continual terror
of the sky falling on their heads.
Somewhat disappointed and not a little bemused,
Alexander dismisses them,
muttering that they think too much of themselves.
The Celts return home, laughing themselves sick.

Nero's Deadline

after Cavafy

When the Delphic Oracle warned Nero:
"Beware the age of seventy three!"
he wasn't unduly concerned.
After all he was only thirty,
plenty of time to prepare
for his future apotheosis.

Now, a trifle weary,
he returns from Achaea.
Deliciously weary,
from a journey devoted exclusively to pleasure:
musical performances, poetry readings, dances,
winning at the Olympic Games, no less.
And, of course, plenty of beautiful Greek bodies.

Meanwhile in Spain,
Galba musters a formidable army,
Galba, seventy-three yesterday.

Goethe in Heaven

No sooner dead than
hurried by Seraphim past
a startled Saint Peter
and swept into the presence of God,
Who, unprompted,
offers Goethe His throne
which Goethe, graciously, accepts.

After Sorescu

A spider's thread
hangs from the ceiling
above my head.

I watch it inch closer
and closer every day.

It looks as if
they're lowering a ladder
from Heaven for me.

Come on soul, up you go,
I'll be right behind.

After Seferis
for Theo

As you sleep,
one eye remains open
to the immense choreographies
of the stars,
one ear alert
to the water fretting
at the rudder.

Danton

for Paul Durcan

He surfaced in a gloomy dream,
without his haughty, brutal air.
Slumped by History's bloody stream,
mourning the loss of Robespierre.

The Sixth Circle

Farinata,
hailing Dante from his burning tomb,
brings me back:
The soaking pits in the steel works,
ten-feet-deep cavities
caked in glistening slag
which we hacked, still hot,
from the steep walls
and shovelled into bins,
until the ladder was lowered
and that infernal foreman
beckoned us
to the surface again.

The Uninvited

Forgotten
in the hallway,
the fully-laden
coat-stand
is crowded
by ghosts,
each longing
to feel
once again
the lovely weight
of clothes.

Holy Souls

November:
here's the ghost of my mother
on her way down to early Mass
followed by the ghost
of her favourite cat
who will wait,
watching for poor ghost mice
from the door of the church,
then follow her
back up the hill
to where the ghost of my father
is preparing breakfast for two
while their real children
sleep fitfully on.

The Poet's Day

Aside from the ticking
of the clock
and a late evening breeze
flicking through the pages
of my next book,
there is only the crystalline memory
of you loosening and tying back
your glorious black hair
on the balcony of the restaurant
earlier today;
everything else fades.

Shift

for Christy Milner

Because he was tired,
he sat down,
his back against the oak tree—
only to wake
to a deep night sky
encrusted with stars;
a sprinkling of rain
cold on his face;
the small glowing hands
on his wrist-watch
spinning backwards.

The Task Laid Aside

after Denise Levertov

Or God
as an old man
living upstairs,
watching old movies
at all hours,
letting His apartment fill
with empty beer cans
which He crunches underfoot
as He shuffles about
muttering in Aramaic.

The Weight of The Word

for Gregory O'Donoghue

Here comes the poet,
inching up Vocabulary Hill,
balanced like a water-carrier
between two full volumes
of the *Shorter Oxford English Dictionary.*

Sea Pictures
for Pilar

ROCHES POINT

As I crest the hill
leading down to the lighthouse,
the landscape unfurls
like a tricolour:
green fields, blue sea,
soaring white clouds;
my flag of convenience.

RED BARN

The squealing of children
embroidered in the thunder
of the rolling surf
as gritty dust devils
whip across the dunes
where young parents
prepare sandwiches,
already sick of one another.

BALLYNAMONA

That Spring afternoon
the sea was rocking itself to sleep
with a muttered litany of complaint
against the cliffs
as we walked barefoot
across the damp sepia wastes
towards the blown-down tower

of the lighthouse,
the giddy blue swell of the sky
lapping at the very shores
of a ghastly daylight moon.

GRABALL BAY

A blustering wind
raises goose-bumps
on the sea's blue-black pelt
as rain swirls in
around the lighthouse
and sweeps along the beach,
spattering the upturned drum
of my mother's red umbrella.

The Moon Rising

after Lorca

When the moon rises,
the church bells hang silent
and shallow mass graves reappear.

When the moon rises,
the river swamps the streets
and the heart is afloat
on an uncharted ocean.

Nobody eats oranges
under a full moon.
One eats fruit
that is green and cold.

When the moon rises,
moon of a thousand murdered faces,
the silver coinage
sobs in your pocket.

Running The Gauntlet

for Tony Sheehan

Taking
a flying leap
from the town's crumbling walls,
you race madly down
through the steep gardens
of Saint Mary's,
hurdle the rhododendrons,
scatter across the gravel,
clamber over the iron gate
and peer back through
the rusty bars—
thirty years on.

My Father Drying My Hair

I have washed my hair
and I am drying it
somewhat distractedly
by the fire.
"Dry it properly,"
my father commands
from behind his newspaper.
I make a half-hearted attempt
but soon lapse into ineffectual dabbing
at its dripping ends.
Eventually, as is his wont,
he takes the towel
and vigorously rubs it dry.
My head, held sweetly
in the busy orbit of his hands,
lulled into a drowsy rapture.

Swimming Out

for M.C.

We spent most of that Summer
under the watchful gaze of the lifeguard.
However, the glowing orange buoy
marking the lobster pots,
easily discernible about a mile out,
haunted our every dreary, shore-hugging swim.
One morning we set out to reach it,
whatever the consequences.
Your brothers joined us
for the first quarter of a mile,
then turned back, warning of dire perils.
We swam on steadily,
two tanned striplings cutting through
the sparkle and glitter
of the early morning ocean,
the tightening silence broken
by the plash plash of our measured strokes
and the flick and ripple
from our trailing feet.
A shoal of sprat brushed past us
at full-pelt and finally unleashed
our pent-up terrors, resulting in
a mad sprint over the last hundred yards to the buoy.
We reached it,
amazed and a little daunted,
by the distance we had covered
and the blue shimmering depths beneath us.
We could just make out the tiny figures
of your brothers running up and down the beach,
waving frantically.
Tired but elated, we began
the long swim home.

Tales from the Microcosm

The late worm
slithers homeward
after a night
on the beer-spattered tiles,
only to meet
the flashing beak
of the stone-cold sober
early bird.

In slow motion
a single drop of rain
belly-flops
and spatters across
an ivy leaf
under which
a housefly
folds away its wings
and awaits the deluge.

If I could lie
(said the earwig)
in the delicate print
your right foot leaves
in the restless sands
beside the oblivious sea,
I could sleep
in the sun-drenched cradle
of your outer ear,
a thousand stories
above the deserted street.

Lines to a Young Girl Eaten by Bears

after the Danish, 9th Century

To make up
for missing your birthday,
your father granted
your fondest wish:
a long hike
through the forest.

Translation and its Discontents

for Belinda McKeon

Stark moonlit silence
the brindled cat is chewing
the nightingale's tongue.

Tree

Eden abandoned,
the Tree of Knowledge laden
with sinister fruit.

Fallen angels perch
in its topmost branches,
shiver in the leaves.

Our father Adam,
we bring you an apple.
Un-name it.

Extract from The Book of Jonah

Now the word of the Lord
came unto Jonah saying:
"Arise and go to Nineveh
and cry out against it,
for their wickedness
is come up before me."

And Jonah said:
"I will, yeah…"

If

after Kierkegaard

If at the bottom of everything
there is only a wild ferment,
a dark power twisting and turning,
spewing up indigestible phenomena,
great or inconsequential.
If an unfathomable, insatiable emptiness
lurks behind the beautiful and the unmentionable.
If one generation rises up after another
like the leaves of the forest,
if one generation follows another
like the songs of the birds in the wood.
If the human race passes through the world
like a ship across the ocean,
or a wind through the desert;

so what.

Climbing Knocknafallia

for Br. Declan

From twelve hundred feet
the sheep paths commence
their final assault on the summit.
The afternoon sunlight
playfully gilds a distant meander
of the Blackwater
as it unfurls towards Cappoquin,
the Monastery bell tolls faintly
through the susurrus of the pine woods.
A steady, agitating breeze
streams over and around you
as you climb,
wearing down your shiny self-esteem,
stripping away layers of hard-won delusion,
fraying at your very notion of self,
until you arrive
trembling with insignificance
amongst the peaks,
reduced to a speck
in the shattering immensities.

Visitation

after Apollonius Rhodius

It was during that sea-grey hour
when darkness seems ready to yield the horizon
to the push of impending day.
We reached the deserted island of Thynias
and clambered down exhausted
onto the welcoming shore,
our hearts at last beginning to lighten.
As if on cue, Apollo, on his way
from Lycia to the slumbering haunts
of those innumerable Hyperboreans,
appeared over our heads.
In his left hand the silver bow,
on his shoulder the full quiver of arrows,
his golden hair framing
his immortal face.
Those of us who saw him
felt a sudden, uncontrollable dismay
and burst into tears.
The whole island trembled
beneath our feet as he passed
and the sea swelled
and crashed onto the beach.
None of us dared to look at him directly:
we stood stock-still, heads bowed,
until he vanished into the brightening distance.

Landscapes

for Jack Healy

MONARD   MIDSUMMER

Having left the party at 3 a.m.,
I took the Killeens road back to the city.
The pale gloom of pre-dawn
cast a ghostly, dream-like shimmer
as if an interface between this world
and another had briefly slid open.
It seemed as if I had only to walk
up the nearby hillside,
into the beckoning circle of trees
and onto the heaving omphaloid mound
to cross over into a shining matrix,
a still-point where past and future
turned tightly, one about the other,
in an infinite moment.

To shake off the plodding tedium
of the roads, we took to the fields.
After clambering gingerly over barbed-wire fences
and deep, booby-trapped ditches,
we emerged scratched and dishevelled
on the very edge of a spectacular valley,
nestling between Rathcooney and Mayfield.
A glorious, forgotten wilderness
in which Artemis herself would have revelled.
A riot of unrestrained bramble, whitethorn, grey nettle,
oxeye daisy, thistle, loosestrife, bindweed, bluebell,
eyebright, red valerian, speedwell, foxglove, deadly
nightshade, milkwort, creeping buttercup, meadow sweet,
meadow rue and thick, waist-high grasses cheerfully ruffled
and unruffled by an impish breeze.
At its bottom a dark stream hurried along
bridged by a fallen oak,
across which ants were carrying
dead and dismembered insects
on small stygian errands.

THE VIEW FROM WHITECHURCH

In a twinkling
the eye takes it all in:
Summer's own lush green country
rolling down through Lisduff and Boolybeg;
sweeping up over the softly rounded hills
of Coolmore, Rahanisky and Ballynahina,
each with its sentinel oak
in stark, majestic silhouette;
past Templemichael's deeply-wooded slopes
and that moth-haunted stretch
of the swiftly descending Glashaboy;
through the blue-shadowed valleys
of Carhoo, Inchacomain and Bawnafinny;
cresting storied Knocknaheeny and leafy Hollyhill,
to light on one glinting window in Frankfield,
faint, forlorn and far away
on the verdant, cloud-capped hills of Cork.

Boy Racers

for Aidan

You'll know them
as they thunder past
in their gold-trimmed chariots,
brandishing ivory-handled whips
across the rippling backs
of their black Spanish stallions,
kicking up the dust
along the Via Sacra
without regard for god or man;
Senators' sons,
every last one.

Cicero Will Get His

after Brutus

I'll grant you our friend Cicero
has done everything with the noblest intentions,
who should know better than I
of his selfless devotion to the Republic.
He is forever banging on
about the Nones of December
when he dispatched the harmless remnants
of the Catiline conspiracy,
whereas we have maintained a dignified silence
with regards to the Ides of March.
He boasts that he, a mere civilian,
faced down the military threat of Anthony.
What good is that if the price
is a successor to Anthony?
I cannot feel any gratitude to a man
who freely deprecates a particular master
but lets slavery itself off the hook.
Long live Cicero, my arse.
Is he not ashamed to think
on his age and rank and past achievements
as he bows and scrapes?
How easily he has been deflected
from fighting the essence of tyranny
by the temporary favour of tyrants.

The Maker

Daedalus,
for all his celebrated ingenuity,
was miffed.
Talos, his nephew and apprentice,
inspired by the jaw-bone of a lizard,
had invented the saw.
Here, at last,
was something with universal application,
unlike labyrinths, hollow wooden cows,
golden honeycombs or countless moving statues.
In a fit of pique he enticed Talos
to view Athens from the summit of the Acropolis
and flung him to his death.

Sensitivity

You say that you fainted
the first time you read Mandelstam,
that only the smelling-salts' effect
of Akhmatova's verse
brought you 'round.

You are too good,
too beautiful for this world.

You should be shot.

A Complaint to the Muse

Too many plain women
are saluting me in the streets.
Too many plain women
are asking me out on dates.
Too many plain women
are ringing me at all hours
to discuss their gloomy half-lives.
Too many plain women
are offering to release me
from the sticky rituals
of solitary sex
in return for a modicum of commitment.
Too many plain women
are trying to convince me
that true beauty, like theirs,
is ultimately internal.
I wish they would stop,
they're playing hell
with my aesthetic.

At North Esk

A distinct chill
in the dusky air
as a moth flits
in a jittery orbit
around the glowing tip
of your cigarette.
Swallows are already
flying South
across the river
to Rochestown
and Casablanca.

The Psychopathology of Everyday Life

after Freud

The old woman,
so small, that when I held
the shop door open for her,
she passed in easily
under my arm.
Somewhere in that split-second,
between the chivalrous act
and the thought
that the ungrateful cow
might be treating me
as a doorman,
I released the heavy,
tightly-sprung door.

I still hear the thump
as it caught her
in the small of her back.

The Drop

after Beckett

Think Michael Collins
plunging through
the open trap
in the flower-strewn
hayloft floor
at Sam's Cross,
to emerge
a moment later
under fire
at Béal na Bláth.

Fart

after Paul Muldoon

The force of it
took him by surprise.
At first he thought
he'd laid one in his drawers
but it was only wind,
in each atom of which,
at that particular moment,
an exquisitely tiny, origamically-folded,
twenty-six-dimensional universe
was unfolding at incredible speed
inside a closed loop
of furiously-vibrating heterotic string,
already primed to expand,
flourish and collapse
in the next ten-millionth of a second.

Still Life

Here's Cézanne,
confined to his sick-bed.
Hat pulled firmly down
pinching his ears,
pipe at full billowing puff
as he sketches the Mont Sainte-Victoire
of his drawn-up, blanketed knees.

And she was beautiful and she was ferociously intelligent

after August Kleinzahler

And I thought
this is where I tell her—
she was on top writhing away
doing that shimmy only she can do
and coming in fits and spurts and starts
now panting now drooling now leaking now grunting
now yelping now farting now belching now speaking in tongues
happily unburdening herself in a fluid litany
of profanities covering the entire patriarchal spectrum
from oppression through objectification to condescension
while I had already lost all purchase
on this level and begun operating tentatively
on the next one up— you know that Tantric stuff—
and I was about to say IloveyouIloveyouIloveyou
alltogetherjustlikethat—
it had been two months since we'd seen each other
and we were going at it hammer and tongs
in her old bed (not the Spartan cot her mother
assigned me with her don't-even-think-of-it look)
it's not as if I was ever reluctant
to spew that perilous incantation
and the flowers fucking wandering fucking lonely
fucking cloudy fucking floating fucking flowers—
so I thought if you say it now she might remember it
when she is being interviewed in her dotage
on *Where is he now and Who was he anyway?*
and it was Christmas I mean jingle bells just unleash
those three tinsled words they will land upright,
well-dressed, house-trained and plausible
on the welcoming porch of her ear
and finally convince her of your undying devotion
but no…

Oasis

after Claudio Magris

Or take
the serene tomb of Gul Baba,
perched on a steep hill
overlooking Budapest
where Death,
giddy with the perfume
of a thousand roses,
is half-inclined
to let you off his hook.

Window

after Milosz

At dawn I looked out
and saw a young apple tree
giddy with translucent blossom.

At dawn I looked out
and saw a young apple tree
laden with glossy fruit.

How many years have passed
since I first looked out,
I cannot tell.

To Myself

after Leopardi

The priest has gone,
taking his precious illusions
wrapped up in his vulture's cloak,
his tail firmly between his legs.
Now you must rest, my Trojan heart.
You have beaten out
a steady rhythm
without a flutter of complaint;
soon you will beat no more.
Life offers nothing in the end
but the certainty of eternal Death.
Its ephemeral delights and torments
are equally meaningless.
Nothingness frets in the shadows,
anxious to erase your fitful span,
as if you had never been.

And Nothing

after Kathleen Jamie

and the road runs out
into the sand
and I kick off my sandals
and walk along the tide-line
and the fishing smacks zigzag
between the breakwater and the horizon,
their wakes crossing and re-crossing,
leaving long foaming gashes on the surface
which gradually disappear;
the sea tending to her own wounds.

Lightning Source UK Ltd.
Milton Keynes UK
UKOW02f0619140116

266345UK00001B/30/P